Everything
You Need to
Know About

Down Syndrome

Kids with Down syndrome are much like everyone else—but not all kids with DS are alike.

Everything You Need to Know About **Down Syndrome**

Mary Bowman-Kruhm, Ed.D.

The Rosen Publishing Group, Inc.
New York

To the members of downsyn@listserv.nodak.edu, whose e-mail posts provide support to families who have a member with Down syndrome and information on DS to the worldwide Internet community.

Thanks to Rick Dill, who provided not only quotes but insight on having an adult child with DS, and to Amy Masser, who graciously spent several hours sharing information with me about Katy, her daughter with Down syndrome.

Very special thanks to Dr. Len Leshin, who readily agreed to review this book and whose thoughtful comments much improved it.

Thank you to the National Association for Down Syndrome (NADS) for its review of the manuscript.

Published in 2000, 2003 by The Rosen Publishing Group, Inc.
29 East 21st Street, New York, NY 10010

Library of Congress Cataloging-in-Publication Data

Bowman-Kruhm, Mary.
Everything you need to know about Down syndrome / Mary Bowman-Kruhm.
    p. cm. — (The need to know library)
Includes bibliographical references and index.
Summary: Examines causes of Down syndrome, new developments in medical treatment, and changes in attitudes toward people who have this condition.
ISBN 0-8239-3767-4
1. Down syndrome Juvenile literature. 2. Mental retardation Juvenile literature. [1. Down syndrome. 2. Mentally handicapped.] I. Title. II. Series.
RJ506.D68B68   1999
616.85'8842—dc21

                                                                                      99-32465

Manufactured in the United States of America

Contents

Introduction

"**M**y sister and I go to the same school. Some kids at school say that my sister is dumb. They call her a sped, which is short for special education.

"But honestly, my sister is not dumb. She knows a lot of things, and has a good sense of humor. She does have problems though, because she can't grow and develop as fast as everybody else. It wasn't anything that she did—she was born that way. Sometimes because of her condition she gets special attention, but most of the time she's just my little sister."

—Daryl, fourteen

Daryl's sister has Down syndrome, or DS for short. DS is a health condition that develops in humans before birth. One can develop DS through his or her lifetime, but only some infants are born with DS. There are special characteristics or traits that are associated with DS. Some of these traits can cause serious health problems. They can also make life more difficult than normal.

A person with DS may have to work harder at things than you do, but he or she is still a valuable member of society. Just like you, he or she has a right to enjoy a happy life. If you know someone with DS, or want to learn more about it, this book is for you. Learning more about Down syndrome can help us to understand the challenges, struggles, and successes of life with DS.

Chapter 1

What Is Down Syndrome?

While Down syndrome causes special traits to develop, people who have DS can be very different from one another. They develop, grow, and learn at their own pace, with their own individual circumstances.

Katie was born with Down syndrome. At age two, she is just beginning to walk. Her mother thinks that Katie's mental abilities are more advanced than her physical coordination. Katie is able to use some words, and when she can't think of a word, she uses hand signals.

Katie loves music. When she hears her favorite songs, she smiles and gets excited. She tries to sing along with the music. She rocks back and forth to the beat while leaning against the sofa.

Children with Down syndrome need special attention, both from parents and educators.

Tyler is also a two-year-old with DS. He crawls to get from one place to another. He uses his arms and upper body to pull himself along the floor. When he wants to move quickly, he rolls. Tyler can now say "dog," "mama," and "dada." When he wants a bottle, he says, "ba-ba." Tyler's older brother used to feed him, but now Tyler tries to feed himself.

Rose is another two-year-old with DS. She has a heart problem that required surgery when she was only five months old. She has hearing problems and frequently develops ear infections. She has already had three treatments for her ear problems and now wears a hearing aid. She doesn't like her hearing aid and often pulls at it. Rose also has trouble with her balance and speech. She has just started to sit up without using her hands for support. When Rose is happy, she babbles and gurgles.

Katie, Tyler, and Rose are quite different from each other. Each has his or her own traits associated with DS. Each has his or her own skills and needs. As they grow older, they will develop into very different people. They have DS, but they are doing what all infants do. They are learning how to move about and how to express themselves. Many infants born

John Down (1828–1896)—Naming Down Syndrome

Historians believe that DS has been around for thousands of years. The condition was first described by Dr. John Langdon Haydon Down in 1866. Up to this time, people with DS and other mental and physical problems were treated very badly. They were sent away to institutions. Many were neglected and their medical problems went untreated.

Dr. Down felt that people with these problems could learn and thrive if given the chance. While studying and training people in the institutions, he discovered that some patients shared the same characteristics. These characteristics, and the condition that causes them, later became known as Down syndrome.

without DS have learned to walk without any help by the age of two. Katie, Tyler, and Rose will also learn, but it will take them a little longer to do so than it would for infants without DS.

The Extra Chromosome

In 1959, Dr. Jerome Lejeune of Paris and Patricia Jacobs of Scotland independently linked the cause of DS to the presence of an extra chromosome. Our bodies are made up of tiny cells that are too small to be seen except through a microscope. In the center of each cell (except red blood cells) there is a nucleus. In this nucleus are genetic materials, or genes. We inherit genes from our parents. Each nucleus holds more than 30,000 genes.

Genes tell each cell how to grow and function. Genes are grouped like beads on a string. Strings of genes are called chromosomes. Normally, every baby gets twenty-three chromosomes from each parent for a total of forty-six. However, babies with DS get an extra twenty-first chromosome from one of their parents. We do not know why.

When there is an extra number twenty-one chromosome, a baby is born with DS. In children with DS, the extra genes on the third twenty-first chromosome disrupt growth and the way the cells function. The baby is born smaller and with fewer brain cells. This process begins long before birth and cannot be reversed.

Genetic Forms of DS

Although all individuals with DS have extra chromosome twenty-one material, there are three types of DS.

◎ Trisomy 21. There is an entire extra chromosome twenty-one in every cell nucleus. Nearly 95 percent of all DS cases are Trisomy 21.

◎ Translocation. The extra twenty-first chromosome material attaches to, or takes the place of, part of another chromosome. This happens in about 3 percent of DS cases.

◎ Mosaicism. An extra whole chromosome is present, but only in some cells. Some cells have forty-six chromosomes and some have forty-seven chromosomes. Only about 2 percent of Down syndrome cases are mosaicism.

Because some cells are normal in mosaicism, some of the physical characteristics of DS may be milder. Otherwise, all three types are much the same in how they affect a baby born with DS.

Is DS Inherited?

Only 3 to 5 percent of all DS cases are inherited. In all other cases, mothers and fathers do not play a role in its development. No one can do anything to prevent it. Children with DS are born to people of all races, in all countries, to both rich parents and poor. It is not caused by the health or diet of the parents or by anything that a mother does when she is pregnant. It is not a disease, and no one can catch it.

Children with DS account for one out of every 800 to 1,000 births. In the United States, about 5,000 babies are born with DS each year. The older a mother is, the greater the chance is of her having a baby with DS. Since most women have children before age thirty-five, most babies (from 75 to 80 percent) with DS are born to young mothers. A forty-five-year-old woman has a one in thirty-five chance of having a baby with DS.

Features of People with DS

Most babies with DS look like other members of their family, but they may also have some of the distinct physical features, or characteristics, that Dr. Down first noted:

- Eyes that slant upward and outward
- Narrow eye openings
- Face that seems to be flattened
- Small head compared to size of body
- Broad feet with short toes
- Ears that are small and set low on head

- ◎ Short arms and legs compared to length of body

- ◎ Broad hand with short fingers and a single crease across the palm

- ◎ Small nose and small mouth, in which the tongue may be too large

- ◎ Lack of muscle tone

- ◎ Ability to extend body joints; extreme flexibility

Not everyone with DS has all of these characteristics. If a baby is born with many, the doctor orders tests to be sure of the correct diagnosis. Sometimes a baby will have so few of these features that only testing will prove or disprove DS. No link exists between DS characteristics and a person's level of intelligence.

DS and Intelligence

Another characteristic or trait of DS is called mental retardation. Mental retardation means a delay, problem, or limitation in the development of mental and social skills. Scientists are not sure exactly how DS causes mental retardation. The extra chromosome of DS somehow disturbs the development and function of the brain.

DS is a common genetic cause of mental retardation. Mental retardation can also be caused by injuries, inherited disorders, and health problems at birth. Other terms, such as mentally retarded, mentally impaired, handicapped, or developmentally delayed are sometimes used to describe someone with mental retardation.

A person with DS can have mild, moderate, or severe mental retardation. Mild retardation can be overcome through special education or training. Severe retardation can make a person completely dependent on others for carrying out simple daily functions. When someone has severe mental retardation, it does not mean that he or she cannot think or feel. It means that he or she has serious limitations carrying out daily tasks or communicating.

Just like you, someone with DS will have their own strengths and weaknesses. Just as you want to be praised for your strengths, so does someone with DS. They may develop at a slower pace, or have mental limitations, but they are not to be judged by those limitations. A person with DS has the right to go to school, to play, and to enjoy life to the best of his or her abilities.

Chapter 2

DS and Health

A newborn baby with DS is in many ways like any other baby. He or she cries, likes to be held, may sleep a lot, needs to eat often, and uses a lot of diapers. But even though babies with DS are very much like other babies, many have problems that may be apparent, or that will begin to develop as time passes.

The truth is that a baby with DS is not always easy to welcome at first. Parents may soon become very tired and stressed from providing the extra care that their child needs. The parents may feel cut off from other family and friends who do not offer sufficient love and support. Raising a child is never easy; it can be even more difficult when a child has DS.

Stages of Growth

The term "developmental delay" may be used to describe children with DS. Children with DS are often slower, or more delayed, than average children in developing skills. Typical children usually master certain skills, such as walking, sitting, talking, and using utensils by a certain age. Children with DS are known to develop these skills somewhat later than children of their own age. For example, typical children are saying their first words between eight and twenty-three months. A child with DS may take up to four years to say his or her first words. This does not mean that a child with DS will never develop the same skills as typical children.

Special Health Problems of Children with DS

Several very specific medical problems are linked with DS. Some of the medical problems that people with DS have include thyroid problems; vision problems; muscle, bone, and joint problems; ear, nose, and throat problems; heart defects; and epilepsy.

Thyroid Function

The thyroid is a gland in the neck that produces the thyroid hormone, which helps the body to grow and function correctly. When the body does not produce enough thyroid hormone, the resulting condition is called hypothyroidism. Hypothyroidism is the most common thyroid problem for those with DS. It can be present at birth or may occur at any age.

Every state in the United States and many other countries routinely screen all newborns for hypothyroidism, which can be particularly hard to detect in babies with DS because the symptoms resemble many other characteristics an infant with DS might have. Doctors suggest that children with DS be checked for thyroid function at birth, six months of age, one year of age, and then once a year thereafter. Problems with thyroid function usually can be treated well with medication.

Vision Problems

About seven out of ten children with DS have some kind of problem with their vision. Children with DS—like all children—should have their eyes checked after their first birthday and then frequently thereafter.

Muscle, Bone, and Joint Problems

Almost all babies with DS have less muscle tone than the average baby. This muscle weakness ranges from mild to severe. Their arms, legs, and neck may be floppy. The child may sit or lie with his or her legs tucked in strange positions. Lack of muscle tone makes the child tire easily. But by the time a child with DS reaches age ten, muscle tone is seldom still a problem.

Anywhere from 10 to 30 percent of children with DS will suffer from what is known as atlanto-axial instability, or AAI. This is when there is a large space between their upper vertebrae, which are the segments of the spinal cord. Children with DS should have neck X rays to check for this problem.

It is not necessary for sports and other physical activities to be limited for children with DS, however, because of mild bone and joint problems. In some cases, certain precautions need to be taken. Parents of children with DS should assure that their children wear all of the correct safety equipment required for each sport in which they participate.

Ear, Nose, and Throat Problems

Some children with DS are more likely to have colds, sinus infections, allergies, asthma, and related problems. This is due to particularly tiny air passages in the ears, nose, and throat. Consistent monitoring by an ear, nose, and throat specialist is important. Such problems also can lead to sleep problems. Sometimes children with DS sleep better after their tonsils and adenoids have been removed. Children with DS also

Although kids with DS sometimes have muscle, bone, and joint problems, they still can engage in a variety of physical activities.

should be regularly tested for hearing problems that may arise.

Heart Defects

About half of all babies born with DS will have heart defects. Such cases need to be referred to a pediatric cardiologist, a doctor who specializes in the heart problems of children. Babies with DS should have tests for possible heart problems soon after birth. If the child has any other health problems that are severe enough to require surgery, a heart specialist should be consulted before the operation.

Epilepsy

Epilepsy is the name given to a number of similar medical conditions that affect the way the body's central nervous system works. The result is seizures of different degrees of intensity. Seizures cause people to lose control of their body and some degree of consciousness, or awareness. A mild seizure might last for only a few seconds; an onlooker may hardly be aware that it happened. Some seizures can last as long as several minutes. The person's body stiffens, and his or her arms and legs jerk. Although this is scary to witness, the person is in no pain while the seizure is taking place.

This does not mean that seizures are not dangerous. People can be injured during seizures—they can fall and hit their head or cut and bruise themselves, for example. Overall, 5 to 10 percent of people with DS have seizures. Adults with DS are more likely to have epilepsy or experience seizures than are children with DS. In most cases, the seizures can be controlled with medicine.

Other Problems

Besides health problems, mental retardation and delays in development cause a number of other problems that can be difficult for children with DS, their families, and their friends to cope with. One of the most difficult of these is with speech.

Speech

We use language both to understand the world around us and to make our needs and wants known. Many young people with DS, even if they do not have hearing loss, are slow to speak.

For children with DS, learning to speak can be a long, frustrating process. It can be equally frustrating for their parents and other family members. Like any toddler, the child with DS needs and wants to make his or her needs understood. When the child cannot do so, he or she may grow angry or frustrated and may act out.

Families can do various things to help make communication easier for a child with DS. A speech pathologist can help families with these issues. A speech pathologist is a specialist who can test, diagnose, and treat speech and communications disorders.

Until the child with DS has a better grasp of verbal communication, many parents use sign language to communicate. When a child wants a glass of milk, the sign for milk helps the parent to understand. Once the child is able to speak, signing is stopped. Until that time, signing provides the parent and child with a way to communicate.

Some parents feel that signing or using word cards in public can make their children look different from the typical child. They insist that the child learn to speak as soon as possible. As with many other child-rearing choices, the family must decide what is right for them and their child.

Family Support

Family support is important for any child, but it is crucial to a child with DS. Among the most important kinds of support the family must provide is taking care of the child's health needs. The family also must help the child to develop a strong sense of identity and self-worth. Since the ability to interact with people begins in the home, the family plays a critical role in helping the child develop to the best of his or her ability. Family members should help a child with DS to develop social skills. Children with DS need to learn how to make wise decisions and how to interact with others. Ultimately the time comes when the child—like any child—must move beyond the family and out into the world.

Chapter 3

A Good IDEA

"*I think that the best thing that I did for my child was to put her in day care that had regular-education kids in it. She was the only child there with a disability. Not only did she learn, but she also taught the teachers, who had been afraid and ignorant about the syndrome.*"

—Renee Mozingo,
mother of a child with DS

IDEA

A number of laws in the United States are designed to help citizens with disabilities. One of these is Public Law 94-142 (PL94-142, for short), which was first passed by Congress in 1975. PL94-142 grants to all children with disabilities the right to public education. This law has been changed several times and is now known as the Individuals with Disabilities Education Act, or IDEA.

Through IDEA all states receive federal money with which they must provide a "free, appropriate education" to children with disabilities. This includes children with DS. The word "appropriate" means that the school a child attends has to be the right one for him or her based on the child's needs and skills.

Evaluation

Before a special-education program and services are provided for a child, he or she must undergo a number of tests. These tests are intended to provide information about an individual child's strengths and needs. The information from the tests is gathered, interpreted, and written up into what is called an evaluation. Based on the evaluation, a team, which includes the child's parents, teachers, and administrators, meets to talk about what program and special services, if any, the child needs to help him or her learn.

Individualized Education Programs (IEPs)

Determining a child's needs is a team decision. If the team feels that a child needs a special program, the law requires the team to draw up an Individualized Educational Program (IEP). The program must be approved by the child's parents and the school system. The child with DS should also be allowed to take part in planning the IEP.

For small children the plan is called an Individualized Family Service Plan, or IFSP. A similar plan for adults is called an Individualized Training Program, or ITP, and prescribes job and living skills for adults.

The law requires the IEP (or IFSP or ITP) to be reviewed each year. After the review, it can be revised or rewritten. The program must spell out the student's learning strengths and weaknesses, the special services needed, special goals and objectives, a time-line for checking on progress, and the people assigned to carry out this program.

Families often feel overwhelmed at such a meeting. Even so, it is important that family members feel free to ask whatever questions they need to. One good idea for the family is to take notes to the meeting on what they want to see happen during the coming year. The wording should be kept simple: "Sue can read about ten words right now. We want her to be able to read one hundred words by June 1." The family should determine what they think will need to be done to reach each goal and ask the staff what methods they will use to reach those goals.

Individualized learning helps people with DS to build on their strengths by setting goals and meeting them.

Families should keep an open mind about what the young person is now able to do, both in and out of the classroom. They should listen to the school staff and be ready to share their own views. They should also include any of the child's personal goals or desires in the program.

Special Services

Special services are often needed to give a child with DS the best chance for success. In fact, at birth a child with DS becomes eligible for services that can help him or her right away. Such services include:

- Speech therapy. Because many children with DS have small mouths, some speech therapists may use sign language if the child is unable to say the words that allow him or her to communicate clearly.

- Physical therapy. A physical therapist works on motor skills such as walking and standing. Problems with muscle tone are often helped by massage.

- Occupational therapy. An occupational therapist works on small motor skills, such as grasping and reaching.

- Mental development. A teacher trained to educate young children with DS can work on a child's skill in understanding concepts (such as big and small, open and closed), shapes, and colors. The teacher also can work on social skills and other areas that affect learning.

School Programs

Until recently, most people did not believe that those with DS could learn. The result was that many children with DS did not get a good education. When they left school, little was expected of them. They stayed at home or lived in institutions with people who had all types of problems. Those with DS seldom interacted with other people in public.

Today, society places more of an emphasis on treating each person with DS as an individual and trying to help him or her live an active, full life—the kind of life that everyone deserves. This means that school is important for the child with DS.

What Kind of Schooling?

Today the parents of a child with DS have many choices about how their child can be educated. For some, home schooling is best even though their child, under IDEA, may attend a public school. These parents feel that they can tailor learning to the child's particular needs.

For other children, a private school or a special program in a public school is needed. There, trained staff structure every part of the day to meet each student's needs. As a child gets older, such programs have the benefit of offering direct training in work skills to help the young person get and hold a job.

For many students with learning problems of any type, the best program allows them to be included in a regular-education classroom. This environment includes all kinds of learners, some who may need special help and many who do not. A second teacher or aide trained to provide special help often works in the classroom alongside the primary teacher. A program like this is called inclusion because the students are included in the regular program. Because two trained adults in the classroom jointly offer their skills and know-how, all students benefit from true inclusion programs.

Some people fear that the inclusion of students who require special help will slow down the progress of other students, but this rarely happens. Instead, studies have shown that *all* students in such groups make great progress, especially in such areas as self-esteem and social skills. It is believed that by welcoming, accepting, and helping children with special needs, other students feel better about themselves.

Inclusion can cause some problems. Teachers may need special training to learn how to help students who learn differently and who have special needs. If the school does not have enough teachers and staff, it can be difficult to provide the necessary help for both typical and special learners. Some of the behavioral characteristics of children with DS can cause teachers, other children, and parents to become upset.

Problems with behavior include acting out, teasing, or hitting. A child with DS may also allow himself or herself to be picked on by a bully or may be stubborn and refuse to follow directions. As is the case with any child, dealing with the situation thoughtfully and patiently is the best method.

What may seem like stubbornness in a child with DS may in fact be an attempt to communicate. Likewise, what seems to be anger in a child with DS may be frustration at his or her own inability to learn or to do something as quickly or as well as other students. The behavior of kids with DS becomes easier to understand when they are included in all aspects of everyday life.

Chapter 4

Growing Up with DS

The school system tries to help Joe. The bus he used to ride had a special harness to keep him safe. He outgrew that, yet he couldn't sit still. His horsing around distracted the driver and bothered the other kids, who made matters worse by teasing him.

The school took Joe off of the bus until the principal worked out a "circle of friends." Now these friends take turns sitting with Joe. They talk quietly and play games. Joe's parents feel that the school did a good job in making the ride comfortable for Joe, and for the other students, too.

Behavior Problems

Any child can be lovable, friendly, kind, selfish, angry, or bratty. Children with DS are no exception. Because children with DS are often delayed in all stages of development, they may be older than the average child when they act a certain way. Most two-year-old children, for example, want their own way and do not like to share. For the child with DS, this stage may not be reached until he or she is older.

Like any other children, those with DS sometimes misbehave. The reason why is not always clear. For the child with DS, inappropriate behavior is often caused by a problem with focusing or by the desire to get his or her own way. Another frequent cause of misbehavior is frustration, caused by the inability to communicate with others. A little patience and understanding on the part of the listener can do much to minimize such frustration.

Problems Focusing

At times everyone finds it difficult to concentrate because of distractions. Children with DS may have a harder time blocking out distractions than most people. For example, a child with DS may find it difficult to pay attention in a classroom covered with bright posters and signs and mobiles that dangle from the ceiling. A student with DS is likely to find such a classroom cluttered and distracting, whereas for other students it simply might be stimulating.

Dealing with Misbehavior

"My son is two and already is starting to throw things. He also doesn't listen to me. He is developing more slowly than other children his age. We have an excellent doctor and a team of specialists—speech, physical therapy, and so on. They all believe that most of this behavior is due to frustration over not being able to do the things he wants to do. He sees other children doing more than he can, and he wants to do those same things but just can't."

—A parent of a toddler with DS

Because many children with DS are delayed in their development, they often find it difficult to deal with the frustration of not getting their way. They also may see other children doing things that they would like to do. This can become frustrating and annoying to the child with DS.

The best way to deal with misbehavior by a child with DS is the same way you would deal with misbehavior by any child. Try to understand the reason for the misbehavior, and work with the child to find a way to keep it from happening again.

Sometimes particular actions seem bad because we do not understand why the person acted that way. Once the reason behind the action is understood, we see the behavior in a different light. Understanding the reason for behavior is not the same as tolerating behavior that is harmful or inappropriate.

Joel's teacher sent home a note that said Joel had pushed a girl, Marie, to the floor. Marie was scared and upset. The teacher said that although Joel didn't seem angry, the teacher, Marie, and her parents couldn't understand his behavior. When Joel's mother questioned him about it, Joel looked puzzled. "I like Marie," he said. "Like her a lot."

Joel's mother figured out that he had meant only to hug Marie. He had pushed her away so hard when he thought the hug should end that she fell to the floor. The incident was an accident, and wasn't done out of anger or aggression. Once his mother understood why Joel had acted the way he did, his family and teacher were able to find a better way for Joel to interact with Marie.

Sometimes a task or lesson must be repeated over and over again before a young person with DS learns the best way of acting in a specific situation. Let's say an eight-year-old child with DS runs away from his parent in a parking lot. A typical eight-year-old could be lectured or punished because he or she would be able to understand the possible dangerous consequences of this action. The child with DS, however, thinks more like a younger child. To stop the child from running away, the parent may have to hold his or her arm and make him or her walk from the car to the store and back, again and again, until he or she understands exactly what kind of behavior is expected.

The Same Standards

Parents, teachers, and friends should expect people with DS to follow the rules of proper behavior. Children with DS should understand that they cannot always get what they want or behave in whatever way suits them.

Justine wanted a new toy. Her mother said, "No, Justine. I do not have money to buy you a toy today. Besides, you have lots of new toys from your birthday last week."

When they returned from the store, her mother noticed that Justine went quietly up to her bedroom and stayed there with the door closed for a long time. After a while, her mother peeked in. Justine was on her bed playing with a toy she had slipped into her pocket while they were in the store.

The Special Olympics is an international competition for developmentally challenged athletes.

Her mother walked Justine back to the store. She made Justine give the toy back and apologize to the store manager.

Exercise and Activities

A good long-term solution to a child's behavioral problems often is to get him or her involved in a fun activity that he or she can handle. Exercise is as important to the overall good health of people with DS as it is to everyone else, so children with DS should be encouraged to take part in physical activities. If young people with DS can do so safely, they should be allowed to play whatever sports they enjoy.

Special Olympics

The Special Olympics is a program that teaches and allows young people with mental retardation to take part in many different kinds of sports. Competitions are held at local, state, and national levels. More than one million athletes throughout the world train and compete. The number of participants is expected to double by 2005.

For many children with DS and other developmental delays, joining the Special Olympics is a good way to spend their time and to take part in athletic activity and competition. As the Special Olympics Oath says, "Let me win. But if I cannot win, let me be brave in the attempt."

Unlike in the past, people with DS today actively participate in social activities and community life.

The Special Olympics offers year-round training and competition in twenty-six different summer and winter sports.

Community

Many people who use the term "inclusion" think of it as something that applies only to school. Inclusion also means being included in the larger community where they live—for example, at a place of worship.

Inclusion can also mean having a job. With a job that provides a paycheck, a person with DS can be independent to the greatest extent possible. Independence can provide each of us with a greater sense of self-worth.

Giving Back to the Community

Some parents encourage their children with DS to visit nursing homes and to do community service work. Such activities serve the community, and they are a good idea for all teens, not just teens with DS. For those with DS, volunteer work can help make them feel more positive about their role in the community. It also provides them with a good way to interact with other people.

Today's young adults with DS are brave pioneers. They are exploring a world that is more inclusive now than it has been throughout history. They are attending schools with both disabled and nondisabled students. They are playing active roles in community life. They are also the first to benefit from new research on DS that has been conducted in recent years.

Chapter 5

The Future for People with DS

*"***W****hen a child with DS turns twenty-one, parents are hit with the reality that our kids will need care and support all their lives. This is where I am now."*

—Rick Dill, parent

Down syndrome is not an illness, such as an infection or disease. It cannot be cured through medicine. It is a genetic condition that—as of yet—cannot be prevented. Babies with Down syndrome will continue to be born. According to the NDSS (National Down Syndrome Society), more than 350,000 Amercian families have a member with DS. The good news is that the outlook is better for people with DS than it has ever been.

Educators and health professionals know the importance of treating DS as early as possible. Family members and peers now have access to several organizations (listed at the back of this book), which also function to improve the quality of life with DS.

Improved Treatments

Advances in treatment and technology promise an improved life for those with DS. In the field of speech, for example, technology has created new equipment to assist people who have limited speech.

Advances in medicine also offer great hope. New surgeries can correct heart, stomach, and intestinal problems. The search continues to find new uses for old drugs and to develop new medications. Because the life expectancy of people with DS is about ten years less than that of the average person, this area of research is extremely important.

Other advances in recent years—such as open-heart surgery, the development of ear tubes (for children with DS who suffer frequent ear infections), and new antibiotics—have done much to improve both the quality and the length of the lives of people with DS.

Lifelong Programs

New programs are opening doors for young people with DS that a few years ago would have stayed tightly shut. Lifelong programs improve the quality of life and allow adults with DS to hold jobs, to live in their own homes, and to contribute to the community.

Most families pay—both in money and in time—to provide for their child with DS, but they often find that extra support is needed from federal, state, and local governments. As they mature, adults with DS need extra help to live in a group home or other housing. They also may need someone to monitor or to assist them with certain activities. This may include help with work, money management, leisure activities, and personal care. Programs that provide these services cost a great deal of money.

"As parents we will not be around forever, and we probably will not have the resources to provide an assured comfortable life for our daughter with DS," parent Rick Dill points out. "We will have to depend upon the system to provide support."

It is little wonder that many parents of children with DS worry about funding their child's continuing care. Even though our laws now provide basic funding, any law, including IDEA, could be changed at any time. In addition, local and state funding for services for people with disabilities vary widely from one place to another, based mostly on the money an area collects in taxes and political and social priorities.

Despite ongoing concerns about money, most people feel that real growth has been made in programs to support people with DS throughout their lives. They point to the increased acceptance of people with DS as reason to believe that the future will be even better.

Public Acceptance and Inclusion

"I want Katy to graduate with functional life skills. I want her exposed to a huge variety of real life and fun skills so that she can pick and choose what she's good at and what she wants to do."
—Amy Masser, mother of a child with DS

Around the world, the unique qualities of people with health conditions are becoming more easily accepted. Some people who are unfamiliar with disabilities may still show discomfort toward people with DS. But more people seem to feel that everyone, including those with disabilities, should be treated fairly.

The next step is full inclusion of those with disabilities as part of the community. People with DS will experience an even greater enjoyment of the huge variety of life experiences if the community can:

◎ **Support funding that will help those with disabilities be successful and independent adults.**

◎ **Hire people with DS who possess necessary job skills.**

◎ Try to accept and understand the special challenges of people with DS.

◎ Avoid discrimination of any kind, especially on the basis of appearance.

◎ Support group homes and apartments so that those with disabilities can live outside their own family in order to live as a welcome and independent member of the community.

Living in Today's World

Bill loved his job cleaning tables at McDonald's. Still, he wondered why some people didn't seem to realize that he had feelings that could be hurt. One customer yelled at him, "Hey, slowboy, hurry up and clean off this table."

A man at the next table said, "Hey, man, leave him alone."

Some adults are not open to having people with disabilities in their lives. They do not want to wait while a person with a disability slowly counts their money at a store. They get impatient when someone with a disability is blocking their way. They laugh and tell jokes about people with DS.

As recently as twenty years ago, when these adults were growing up, people with disabilities such as DS

Acceptance in the workplace enables adults with DS to live successfully on their own.

were kept away from the general public. These adults have little or no experience with being around people with DS. They do not know how to interact with people with DS, and they don't feel comfortable doing so. These older generations were not exposed to the concept of inclusion.

Although inclusion seems to work while children are young, most young people go their own way in their teens. Children with DS often find themselves more and more isolated and alone as they become young adults. Many parents of children with DS find that regardless of whether their children have been part of inclusion programs in school, they are likely to become increasingly isolated from the ages of thirteen to twenty-one. Inclusion at these ages may seem forced or token. This is something parents have to recognize and deal with.

Most parents of children with DS find their child's isolation frustrating and work to keep their child involved in community life. After all, people with DS have the same feelings, drives, and urges that most everyone has. They want to go to school parties and dances, to join clubs and community groups, and to do everything that other young adults do. They want to have friends as well as boyfriends and girlfriends. This leads to all the usual concerns about sexual behavior, including the dangers of sexually transmitted diseases and unwanted pregnancy. These risks may be even

People with Down syndrome enjoy dating and romantic relationships just like everyone else.

greater for children with DS if they lack the necessary social skills to successfully negotiate potentially risky situations. The need for friendship, acceptance, and intimacy, combined with difficulty in communicating and setting boundaries, can make romantic and sexual relationships especially troublesome for teens with DS.

Most parents of adult children with DS understand that their children have sexual needs and desires. But pregnancy, in particular, is a great concern. Many parents of children with DS feel that the problems that might result from their child having and rearing his or her own children are simply too great to justify the risk. According to the National Association for Down

Syndrome (NADS), there is only one documented case of a man with DS fathering a child. Women with DS can have children, but the child has a 35 to 50 percent chance of being born with DS. For these reasons, many parents advise young adults with DS not to have children. Regardless of parental concern, many young adults with DS form meaningful relationships. Some find love and marry. Those that do not find relationships should be encouraged to seek out other sources of enjoyment. They can take classes, register to vote once they're eighteen, and explore life opportunities.

No one with DS, child or adult, should live a life of isolation. Unfortunately, many people with DS withdraw into isolation as they age. This does not have to happen if people are willing to allow them into their lives. A life apart can easily be turned into a life of inclusion.

Chapter 6

Down Syndrome Up Close

*T*he group home counselor sat with three young adults with DS at a table in the middle of the fast-food restaurant. She watched as other teens, just out of school and eager to eat, headed toward the empty seats near their table. When the teens saw her group, they moved to a table across the restaurant. She put down her burger and sighed.

Many of us keep our distance from someone who looks or seems different from ourselves. At work or at school, we prefer to interact with those we know rather than someone whom we think is not like us. We create a comfortable, but small and limiting, environment. While this is a normal response, it shouldn't keep you from getting to know someone with DS.

51

What We Say Matters

The way that we talk about other people matters. The way people talk about you matters to you, doesn't it? People with disabilities, including people with DS, are no less sensitive. Using the wrong words can cause a person and his or her family a lot of pain.

What some people say about people with DS often reflects a negative attitude toward them. "Idiot" is a term first used as one of scorn and abuse by the ancient Greeks. It later came to mean someone who was considered to be mentally slow—not particularly bright, dimwitted, or retarded. None of these terms should be used today, particularly to describe a person with a disability or DS, neither should other negative terms that were once commonly used, such as "sped." These labels, in fact, show the ignorance of the speaker. One of the best ways to refer to a person with a disability is to use his or her name.

Think of someone with DS as a person first, then as someone with DS. The best way to refer to someone with DS—or to anyone with a problem—is to put the person before the disability. By doing this you show that you think of him or her first and foremost as a person.

The best rule is to treat someone as you would like to be treated. You would probably prefer for someone to call you by your name, rather than yelling physical descriptions like, "Hey, big feet!"

More Alike Than Different

Joan stood in the checkout line with Richie, her twelve-year-old son with DS. The cashier counted out Joan's change and said, "Ten dollars and one cent."

"Too much. Dime, not penny."

"Goodness, I did give your mom the wrong change!" said the cashier. She looked at Joan and smiled. "It's wonderful that he caught that. Just like a real person."

The woman at the checkout counter thought she was paying Richie a compliment, but she really was not. Her intentions might have been good, but she hadn't given what she said much thought. If asked, could she have listed any reasons why a person with DS was something other than a "real person"? Note that throughout this book you've read "child with DS," not "DS child." People with DS are real people—as real as anyone else.

How to Act and What to Say

Suppose you are watching your sister play soccer. A little boy with DS and his mother are standing next to you. The little boy smiles at you. He reaches into his pocket and takes out a pack of gum. He says, "Gum," and holds a stick in his hand for you to take. This is a tricky situation that requires an appropriate response. Just how do you treat someone with DS?

The best advice can be summed up in one sentence: Treat someone with DS (or any disability) as you would anyone else. You do not need to go out of your way to talk or interact with him or her. Just because a child has a disability does not mean that you should pay more attention to him or her. At the same time, be polite. Just because someone has a disability does not mean that you should pay less attention to him or her, either.

Friendly, But Not Too Friendly

Many people with DS try to become instant friends with others. Their families worry that they will become friends with someone who will hurt them in some way. They try to teach children with DS that talking to strangers is not a good idea, and they prefer that strangers not respond to their children in a super-friendly way. If someone with DS tries to become too friendly, the best thing to do is what you would do with any stranger: Be polite, but not overly friendly.

So what can you say? To a toddler, you might say, "Do you like to watch that big yellow bird on television?" You might ask someone older, "What's your favorite TV show?" And you can say to anyone, "Isn't the warm weather wonderful? I sure hope it lasts."

What NOT to Say to a Family

Family and friends of children with DS get tired of hearing people say things that—although meant to be kind—often hurt. Here are a few of them:

- ◎ **"I know someone who has DS, and he's so lovable." (This is offensive in two ways. DS is not an illness, like the flu, that someone has. It is better to say that you know someone with DS. And lovable is not how people with DS always are.)**

- ◎ **"They're really sweet kids, aren't they?" (This separates the child from "normal" children.)**

- ◎ **"He'll be all right." (The child is all right—right now. He or she won't or can't get over DS as if it is a passing thing.)**

- ◎ **"She looks like she has just a little Downs." (If she was born with that extra chromosome, she has DS; it is not a disease in which someone has a little DS or a lot.)**

Here are some things you can say or do:

◎ "I'm going to play catch with my sister. Can your son play, too?" (If the child is older, you could talk directly to him.)

◎ If you know the child, simply say, "Hello." (If he or she is with a parent, explain that you know the child from school, or Little League, etc.)

◎ "Wow! What a pretty smile she has!"

Your comments should say something about the child as an individual person. Treat the person with DS as you would anyone else—as an individual deserving of respect.

What is the best way to do that? Include the person with DS. You can sit with him or her at lunch or bring the person into your conversations with other friends. Say hello when you see him or her at school or other places. Call him or her up some time, even if it is simply to say hi. Treat a person with DS the same way that you would treat anyone else—the way that you would like to be treated.

Glossary

annual review A yearly meeting to go over the Individualized Educational Plan (IEP).

assessment Testing of a student to decide if there is a need for special-education services.

developmental delay (mental retardation) Characterized from birth or infancy by intellectual ability that is severely below average.

epilepsy Name for various disorders characterized by disturbances in the central nervous system that result in seizures and convulsions.

genetic (or hereditary) conditions Specific conditions, syndromes, or diseases directly attributable to a child's genetic inheritance from his or her biological parents.

home schooling Schooling that takes place exclusively in the home rather than in a school, usually under the direction of a parent.

IDEA Abbreviation for Individuals with Disabilities Education Act.

IEP Abbreviation for Individualized Educational Plan.

inclusion Education of a student with special needs in a general-education classroom.

ITP Abbreviation for Individualized Training Program; similar to the IEP, but spells out specifically what is needed to provide an adult with work and living skills.

PL94-142 Abbreviation for Public Law 94-142, which was the first legislation in the United States that provided for the public education of all children with disabilities.

self-contained class A special classroom, usually within a school building, where students with special needs spend most of the school day.

special services Services other than educational ones for a person who has been assessed and found to need those services. Examples include speech and language therapy, occupational therapy, physical therapy, and other forms of social work.

speech pathologist Someone who is trained to work with people who have problems with speech and/or language. A speech pathologist might help a person who is speech impaired find different ways to communicate with others, as well as improve his or her speech.

Where to Go for Help

The Arc of the United States
1010 Wayne Avenue, Suite 650
Silver Spring, MD 20910
(301) 565-3842
e-mail: info@thearc.org
Web sites: http://www.thearc.org
Resources and advice: http://www.thearclink.org
National publications desk (books and videos):
http://www.thearcpub.com

The Canadian Down Syndrome Society (CDSS)
811-14 Street Northwest
Calgary, AL, Canada T2N 2A4
(403) 270-8500
Web site: http://www.cdss.ca

The Council for Exceptional Children (CEC)
1110 North Glebe Road, Suite 300
Arlington, VA 22201-5704
(888) CEC-SPED (232-7733)
(703) 620-3660
e-mail: service@cec.sped.org
Web site: http://www.cec.sped.org

Down Syndrome Research Foundation (DSRF)
1409 Sperling Avenue
Burnaby, BC, Canada V5B 4J8
(888) 464-DSRF (3773)
(604) 444-3773
Web site: http://www.dsrf.org

National Down Syndrome Society (NDSS)
666 Broadway
New York, NY 10012
(800) 221-4602
(212) 460-9330
Web site: http://www.ndss.org/main.html

Special Olympics
1325 G Street NW, Suite 500
Washington, DC 20005
(888) 700-8585
(202) 628-3630
Web site: http://www.specialolympics.org

For Further Reading

Anderson, W., S. Chitwood, and D. Hayden.
*Negotiating the Special Education Maze: A Guide
for Parents and Teachers*. Reston, VA: Council for
Exceptional Children, 1997.

Bowman-Kruhm, Mary, and Claudine Wirths. *Coping
with Discrimination and Prejudice*. New York: The
Rosen Publishing Group, Inc., 1998.

Bryan, Jenny. *Living with Down Syndrome, Volume 6*.
New York: Raintree Steck-Vaughn, 1999.

Girod, Christina M. *Down Syndrome*. Farmington
Hills, MI: Gale Group, 2001.

Selikowitz, M. *Down Syndrome: The Facts*. New York:
Oxford University Press, 1997.

Westridge Young Writers Workshop. *Kids Explore the
Gifts of Children with Special Needs*. Santa Fe, NM:
John Muir Publications, 1994.

Index

About the Author

Dr. Mary Bowman-Kruhm is a writer and an educator. She is the author of more than twenty books for teens, as well as numerous articles for professional journals and magazines.

Photo Credits

Cover and pp. 2, 40, 47 © Greenlar/The Image Works; pp. 21, 38 © Lawrence Migdale/Photo Researchers, Inc.; p. 28 © Richard Hutchings/Photo Researchers, Inc.; p. 9 © Ron Chapple/FPG International; p. 49 © Michael L. Palmieri/The Ames Tribune.

Series Design

Thomas Forget

Layout

Hillary Arnold